D-Day—
Omaha Beach

D-Day—
Omaha Beach

Milton J. Shapiro

David McKay Company, Inc.
New York

Photos courtesy of U.S. Army

Copyright © 1980 by Milton J. Shapiro

All rights reserved, including the right to reproduce this book, or parts thereof, in any form, except for the inclusion of brief quotations in a review.

Library of Congress Cataloging in Publication Data

Shapiro, Milton J
D-Day—Omaha Beach

Includes index.
SUMMARY: Discusses the invasion by the mightiest armada in the history of warfare that marked the beginning of the end for Hitler's Third Reich.
1. World War, 1939-1945—Campaigns—France—Normandy—Juvenile literature. 2. Operation Overlord—Juvenile literature. [1. World War, 1939-1945—Campaigns—France—Normandy. 2. Operation Overlord] I. Title.
D756.5.N6S48   940.54'21   80-7962
ISBN 0-679-20575-6

1 2 3 4 5 6 7 8 9 10

Manufactured in the United States of America

Contents

1. The Mighty Armada 1
2. Bloody Omaha 10
3. "Lead the Way, Rangers!" 23
4. The Tide Turns 37
5. The End of the Beginning 52
   Index 56

This is the view German gunners had from their pillbox flanking the beach. Because American troops found no place to take cover here, they were easy targets for murderous machine gun crossfire.

1
The Mighty Armada

In the predawn darkness of a morning in June 1944, the mightiest armada in the history of warfare plowed through the choppy gray waters of the English Channel, heading for the northern coast of France. Some five thousand ships were in this awesome convoy—huge battlewagons, sleek cruisers, swift destroyers, bulging troopships, rusting cargo carriers, landing craft for troops and tanks, scudding gunboats, and PT boats. All had their bows pointed toward the beaches of Normandy, just twenty miles away across the dark waters.

In the crowded holds of the transports, thousands of combat troops readied themselves for the battle soon to come. Weapons were cleaned and checked. Ammunition was doled out. Maps were studied again and again. Orders were quietly given. Some men whiled away those tense moments before dawn by swapping stories and jokes, by playing cards, or by writing letters to mothers, wives, friends, and sweethearts.

For many of those thousands, it would be their last letters, their last hands of cards, their last rounds of jokes. For many of those men, death waited on the beaches; they would never see another dawn. More men would be wounded, would feel the numbing, hammer blow of a bullet, the searing agony of hot shrapnel cutting into flesh. And yet, many would still live to fight another day.

In the darkness across the Channel, entrenched in the bluffs overlooking the beaches, the Germans waited. Unaware of the approach of the Allied convoy, but knowing that the enemy must soon come, these men of the *Wehrmacht*, or the War Machine, slept an uneasy sleep. All night hundreds of bombers had been overhead. The earth had trembled in their wake. Now it was quiet—too quiet.

Men on guard duty nervously fingered the triggers on their weapons. In concrete bunkers and observation posts, lookouts peered through high-powered binoculars into the darkness, straining for any sign of the enemy. Would this be the morning when the British and the Yanks would attack? The weather reports had predicted strong winds and rough seas. Surely there would be no invasion this morning!

Within hours, many of these men would be dead, crippled, or wounded—shot, shelled, or burned to a crisp by flamethrowers as they cowered in their bunkers. The lucky ones would be those who had time to throw up their hands and shout "Kamerad!" before being cut down by a GI or a Tommy.

This was D-Day, the 6th of June, 1944—the day when the combined forces of the British, Canadian, and American armies began their assault on Adolph Hitler's *Festung Europa*, or Fortress Europe. This was the day that marked the beginning of the end for the Third Reich, a regime Hitler had boasted would last for a thousand years.

All over Europe, the vaunted German armies were in retreat. Thrown out of Africa and Sicily by American and British armies, they were falling behind in Italy, fighting desperately to hold onto Rome. On the eastern front, they were being pushed back into Poland by the Russians; entire divisions were being cut to pieces. Day and night, British and American bombers thundered over Germany, dropping thousands of tons of bombs on German cities, railroads, and industries.

Now it was time for the final chapter. The Allied Chiefs of Staff, under their Supreme Commander, Gen. Dwight D. Eisenhower, had planned this day for many months. There could be no possible compromise with Hitler, no armistice, no cease-fire, no negotiations. Germany had to be defeated on the battlefield—forced to surrender unconditionally.

To accomplish this, Allied armies had to invade occupied France, drive the German armies back and crush them on the soil of their own homeland. The invasion, code-named "Operation Overlord," was timed for either June 5th or 6th, when conditions would be just right for the attack: a moon to aid the night drop by paratroopers; and a low tide in the morning that would help the troops across the Normandy beaches that were code named and assigned to specific units. The beaches called Juno, Sword and Gold were the targets of the British and Canadians. Utah and Omaha were the names given to the two beaches assigned to the American forces. Utah would be hit by the 4th Infantry Division, Omaha by Regimental Combat Teams of the 1st and 29th Infantry Divisions, assisted by the 2nd and 5th Ranger Batallions.

The plan was this: At midnight on the night before the invasion, British and American paratroopers would drop behind the German lines. Their mission: to seize important strong points, such as bridges and crossroads; to set up roadblocks and stall enemy reinforcements

Assault units of the 29th Division wading ashore on section of Omaha Beach, code named "Beach Dog Green."

Their landing craft sunk, these men of the 29th Division took to a rubber raft and made it safely to the beach despite enemy sniper fire.

rushing to the invasion beaches, and to cause as much havoc and confusion in the enemy ranks as possible.

Then, at 6:30 the next morning, the first wave of infantry would charge from their landing craft and attack the beach defenses. Supporting the infantry would be tanks and demolition engineers. An hour later, the support units would begin landing more tanks, more infantry, heavy weapons units, and field artillery. With the beaches secured, these men would begin to push inland and clear the way for the many divisions that would follow in the days and weeks to come.

While all this planning was going on at Allied Headquarters in England, the Germans were not completely asleep. Field Marshal Erwin Rommel, the famous "Desert Fox," knew an invasion was inevitable. He, too, had been preparing for many months for D-Day. All along the French coast, thousands of German soldiers and laborers had been building defenses—an Atlantic Wall, the Germans called it—which would stop the Allies.

In the water itself were thousands of obstacles: a maze of X-shaped concrete and steel structures, capped with mines that would explode on contact. These were designed to blow up any landing craft hitting them, or at least trap the boats and halt them long enough for the German guns to zero in on them and blow them up.

The sands of the beaches were sown with more than a million mines. Some were designed to blow up tank treads, others to blow off a man's legs if he stepped on one. Still others were made to jump into the air and explode waist high. Beyond the sands, where the beaches ended abruptly in a seawall and steep bluffs, stood double aprons of barbed wire. Built into the bluffs were concrete bunkers and pillboxes, bristling with machine guns and antitank guns.

On top of the bluffs were more bunkers and pillboxes, their guns pointing straight down to the beaches, giving

These obstacles were set all along the beach to block landing craft. Many of them were wired with mines that exploded on contact.

German soldiers plant anti-personnel mines in the sands along Omaha Beach.

Troops of the 1st Infantry Division wading ashore on D-Day at Omaha Beach.

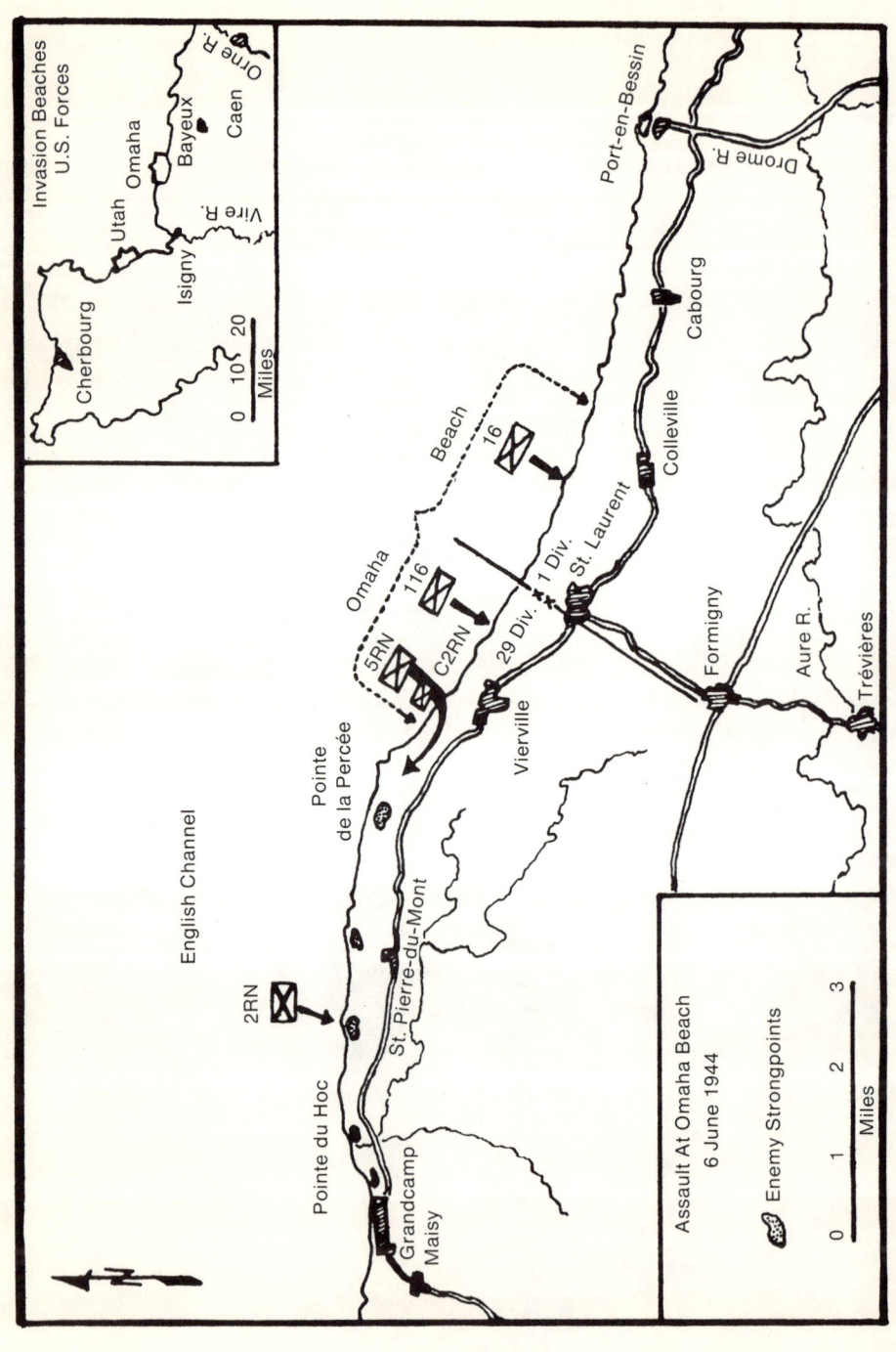

the Germans point-blank overlapping fields of fire. These strong points were connected by a complex series of communication trenches, all well protected behind barbed wire. Well dug in all along the coast, the Germans were confident that they could repel any invading force.

However, Rommel had no more dreams about Germany winning the war. All he hoped for was the chance of a negotiated peace with the Allies before Germany was destroyed completely. He believed that if he could stop the coming invasion right on the beaches, there was such a chance, especially if the German generals could get together and rid themselves of Hitler. If this was impossible, then all was lost.

On April 22nd, 1944, Rommel issued the following field order: "We must succeed, in the short time left until the large offensive starts, in bringing all defenses to such a standard that they will hold up against the strongest attack. Never in history was there a defense of such an extent with such an obstacle as the sea. The enemy must be annihilated before he reaches our main battlefield."

So the stage was set. And on the morning of June 6th, while American and British paratroopers were already in action behind the German lines, the mighty Allied armada dropped anchor twelve miles off the Normandy shores and prepared to launch the attack. Dawn came at 3:30 A.M. The troops emerged from below deck and began to load into their landing boats. In three hours, all five invasion beaches would be ablaze with the fire of battle. Each beach would see its own bitter battle fought, but none would be so terrible as the struggle on that four-mile crescent of sand, called Omaha Beach. Before sunset, that beach would be cursed forever by the American troops who survived its hell. And it would be remembered by them as well as by history as "Bloody Omaha."

2
Bloody Omaha

The sea was rough—much too rough for the small assault craft, as they scurried like a swarm of water beetles toward the shore. The boats pitched and rocked, their square jaws butting into every wave. Water poured over the gunwhales, soaking the men to the skin, as they huddled together, shivering from the cold and from nervous tension. Many of the men became seasick.

The noise was deafening. The diesels of the boats throbbed and roared in the men's ears. Shells screamed and crashed, as the big guns of the fleet sent salvo after salvo pounding into the German positions on the bluffs. Overhead, Lancasters and Liberators, Spitfires and Mustangs shuttled back and forth over the beaches, bombing and strafing the hills. It seemed to the men in the boats that no enemy could possibly survive such a bombardment; at least, that's what they hoped.

Now the boats were just a thousand yards from shore. And, still the German guns were silent. Then

A German gun emplacement above Omaha Beach.

disaster struck Omaha Beach. The heavily laden boats, riding deep in the heavy seas, began to founder, taking on too much water. Men bailed out frantically using their helmets. Some of the boats began to sink. The men struggled in the sea, weighed down by equipment and ammunition. Their pitiful cries for help went mostly unanswered. The orders were—invade without stopping for casualties. A few men, however, were picked up, but many perished.

In the waters off the 1st Division's sector of the beach, twenty-nine amphibious tanks of the 741st Tank Battalion were launched. In short order, they were swamped by the waves. Their canvas water wings were ripped to shreds; support struts were broken. Water flooded the engine compartments. Twenty-seven tanks went down. The men came scrambling up out of the hatches, leaping into the sea. Some of them made it to shore, along with two crippled tanks. The rest drowned in their vehicles.

The first wave of boats was barely 400 yards from shore when the German guns opened fire. Artillery and mortar shells came crashing down, sending geysers of water shooting into the air. One boat was hit, then another. Chunks of metal and parts of bodies flew skyward, then splashed back into the sea. Machine guns from the pillboxes started chattering, the bullets clanging against the ramps and sides of the boats.

Bobbing about on the surf near the shore, trying to find a path through the obstacles, the boats were sitting ducks for the German gunners. Demolition men leaped from the boats into neck-high water and tried to blow a way clear. They were picked off, one by one.

About 100 yards from the beach, the boats ground to a halt on sandbars. The ramps were lowered. The men of the 1st and 29th Divisions leaped forward—and found themselves in water that was almost above their heads. As

A German 88 shell bursts amid infantry of the 1st Division on Omaha Beach.

Amphibious tanks, using 105mm howitzers, prepare to take on German 88's at Omaha Beach.

if this had been a signal which the enemy was waiting for, the ramps were instantly enveloped in a murderous cross fire from the German guns. Overloaded with equipment, stiff from their voyage, seasick, floundering in the water—the men never had a chance.

Company A of the 116th Regimental Combat Team, 29th Division, were headed for the beach at a sector code named "Dog Green." As the company's six assault boats lowered their ramps, machine gunners on the cliffs fired straight down on them. Company Commander Capt. Taylor N. Tellers and thirty men on his boat were killed before they could even reach the sands.

Lt. Edward Tidrick, a platoon leader, jumped from the ramp of his boat into the water, shouting for his men to follow him. A bullet caught him in the throat. He managed to wade through the surf and flop on the sand near one of his men, Pvt. Leo J. Nash. Raising himself on one elbow, the lieutenant gasped to Nash, "Advance with the wire cutters!" It was futile. Nash had no wire cutters. But in giving the order, the lieutenant had made himself a target. He was killed when a machine gunner on the cliff caught him with a burst of fire from head to foot.

The other four boats of the company suffered similar fates. A boat filled with medics, who were trying to pick up wounded men floating in the water, was raked by machine gun fire that killed or wounded every single man in the section. As the troops were cut down while leaving the ramps, others threw themselves over the sides, hoping to escape the cross fire. Men were all around the boats now, struggling with their equipment, trying to stay afloat, while machine gun and rifle bullets flicked the water and mortar shells burst amongst them. As they slipped beneath the waves and died, their bodies soon bobbed back to the surface and floated back and forth with the tide.

Just ten minutes after the ramps had been lowered,

Company A of the 116th ceased to be a fighting unit. Every officer was dead except for one, Lt. Elijah Nance, and he was lying on the beach, shot twice. Every sergeant was either killed or wounded. As far as the survivors of Company A were concerned, the invasion had become a struggle to stay alive. Leaderless, unable to shoot back at the unseen enemy in their pillboxes, the infantrymen tried to save themselves and their wounded comrades.

The men in the water pushed the wounded ahead of them while wading to shore in order to save them from drowning. Those who safely reached the sands crawled back and forth into the surf, pulling men onto the beach. In the process, many were killed or wounded by snipers and machine gun fire. By the time Company B boats came in behind the A boats, barely a dozen men in a company of almost two hundred were fit for duty.

Company B did not fare much better than A. The ramps of the assault boats were let down seventy-five yards from the beach. The first man out was the Company Commander, Capt. Ettore V. Zappacosta. He got ten yards through the water when a machine gun burst caught him. "I'm hit!" he yelled. A young medic named Kenser called out, "Hang on, try to make it in!" Zappacosta disappeared beneath the waves. Kenser leaped in after him and was shot dead. Then Lt. Tom Dallas jumped into the water. He, too, was killed. The fourth man out was Pfc. Robert L. Sales, a radio operator. Loaded down with equipment, he tripped coming out of the ramp and fell headlong into the water. That saved his life. Every man in the boat who followed him was either killed or wounded. Sales was the only man to get as far as the beach unhurt.

All along the four-mile stretch of Omaha Beach there was death and confusion. Boats were sent to the wrong beaches. Equipment was sunk or abandoned. Men, struggling in the pounding surf, threw away their weapons and

A dead German soldier lies outside his pillbox on Omaha Beach.

Assault troops of 3rd Battalion, 16th Infantry Regiment, 1st Division, landing on Omaha Beach on D-Day.

helmets in order to stay afloat. Blazing hulks of assault craft littered the shoreline. The incoming tide caught the wounded at the edge of the waterline and sucked them back into the sea. Medics moved among the line of bodies that were pinned down on the sands by the enemy fire and sorted out the dead from the living. Many of them were also cut down by a hail of bullets.

In the 1st Division's sector, where the 16th Regimental Combat team tried to land, German mortars and artillery took a heavy toll in men and boats. Since most of the assault companies landed in the wrong place on the beach, all semblance of coordination was lost. Company E lost 105 men in the water. In the command boat, only twelve of the thirty-six men on board survived.

Company F, too, was badly hit. The command boat lowered its ramp seventy-five feet from shore. As the men started out, a mortar burst killed the executive officer, Lt. Howard Pearre, and several others. Then a machine gun burst killed the company's own machine gun leader, S. Sgt. William A. Miller, two squad leaders, Sgts. Robert Price and Rodney Chase, and two gunners.

By the time the men of the command boat reached the water's edge, only seventeen of the thirty men were left, and seven of those were wounded.

The No. 1 assault boat of this company hit a sandbar fifty yards from shore. Machine gun bullets beat a tattoo on its metal sides. The men yelled for the ramp to be lowered. When it came down, they leaped into neck-deep water. Some were killed on the ramp, others as they tried to wade to the beach. The section leader, Lt. Aaron Dennstedt, made it safely to the shoreline. There, he turned and yelled for his men to keep moving. At that moment, a sniper shot him through the head. Of the thirty-one men in that boat, only fourteen survived.

The second section assault boat, commanded by Lt.

Medics of the 2nd Battalion, 16th Infantry Regiment, attend a badly wounded soldier as other wounded men wait for evacuation to hospital ships.

Bernard J. Rush, beached about thirty yards from land. There, the water was shallow and the men could run through it. But machine gun and mortar fire quickly found them. The BAR (Browning Automatic Rifles) specialists were caught by a mortar burst. Pfc. Frank DeBellis was killed at once. Pfc. George Bert had his right leg blown off. Despite the wound, he crawled 100 yards up the beach for cover. But since there were no medics nearby, he bled to death.

Of the thirty-one men in this boat, twenty made it to the beach; ten of those were wounded.

A few minutes after the ramps went down on Company F's boats, only two officers were capable of command. All units suffered severe casualties. Less than half of the company was in any condition to fight.

At 7:00 A.M., the second wave of assault troops began arriving at Omaha Beach. Instead of firmly held positions and beaches cleared of the enemy, the men found a shambles. No objectives had been taken. The survivors of the first wave were still at the water's edge; a few had gotten as far as the seawall.

Struggling past the bodies of the dead and the wounded, the second wave from the two assault divisions tried to cover the 300 yards or so of sand to reach the bluffs. Soon, these men, too, were pinned down by the deadly accurate fire of the Germans. The third wave of troops arrived, then the fourth. The beaches were jammed with assault craft, burning hulks, abandoned equipment, the dead, the wounded, and confused combat infantrymen who were waiting for someone to tell them what to do. The invasion came to a halt at Omaha Beach.

The command groups of both Regimental Combat Teams decided they had better get up there and find out what was going on. The Commanding Officer of the 116th RCT, Col. Charles Canham, along with his staff

Wounded and exhausted men of a troop of the 1st Division take a few moments' break under the shelter of a sea wall on Omaha Beach.

and Brig. Gen. Norman D. Cota, assistant division commander of the 29th, headed for "Beach Dog White." They were all in one landing craft.

The command group of the 116th RCT went forward in two boats. The lead boat was almost completely demolished. But the Commanding Officer, Col. George A. Taylor, got ashore safely in the second boat.

Back on Beach Dog White, the boat carrying Col. Canham and Gen. Cota grounded on a sandbar seventy-five yards from shore. The ramp went down, and the men leaped into waist-high water. Despite the hail of bullets all around them, the group made the beach with just one casualty.

What the officers saw on Omaha Beach dismayed them. It was obvious that despite all the naval and aerial bombardment, the Germans had not been seriously weakened. There was no sign on the beaches of any damage at all—no bomb craters, no demolition of beach obstacles or installations. The concrete bunkers and pillboxes, built into the bluffs and on top of the bluffs, continued to pour down a relentless volley of fire.

There was another problem, too, one which they did not yet know about. According to Allied Intelligence, Omaha Beach was defended by the Germans' 716th Infantry Division. Unknown to Intelligence, however, the crack 352nd Infantry Division had just moved into the area on anti-invasion maneuvers, proving that the Germans were much better prepared than had been expected.

On the beach, the command officers tried to break the paralysis gripping the troops. Col. Canham moved among the men, looking for the officers of his 2nd Battalion, trying to get some kind of movement going. As he reached the area where the survivors of C Company were pinned down, he was hit in the wrist by a machine gun bullet. He stuck a bandage on the wound and kept on with his patrol, urging his men forward toward the shelter of the seawall.

Col. Taylor, in the 1st Division sector, found his men in a similar state of disorganization and paralysis. Exposed on the beach, using anything they could find for protection against the murderous fire—even dead bodies—the men were suffering further casualties from mortar and artillery fire.

Standing up in full view of the enemy, Col. Taylor shouted to his men: "Two kinds of people are staying on this beach, the dead and those who are going to die. Now let's get the hell out of here!"

3
"Lead the Way, Rangers!"

The Rangers had a special mission on D-Day. On the right flank of Omaha Beach stood a rocky cliff called Pointe du Hoc. This 100-foot high cliff, surrounded on three sides by water, had been transformed into a massive fortress. Six huge, 155 mm long-range howitzers were casemated on the cliff in concrete pillboxes with walls six-feet thick. This battery was one of the most dangerous elements of the German defenses in the assault area. With a range of fifteen miles, the 155's could devastate anything that moved, not only at Omaha Beach but at Utah Beach as well.

Those big guns had to be silenced—and quickly.

The Germans considered the position to be almost impregnable, especially from the seaward side. Below the cliff was a narrow strip of beach without the slightest cover for assaulting troops. Nevertheless, both flanks of the cliff were defended by a series of machine gun nests. On the landward side a mine field, barbed wire, and a

One of the German gun emplacements on Pointe du Hoc knocked out by the Rangers.

series of strong points and entrenchments protected the men against attack. It was estimated that about 125 infantry and 85 artillerymen of the 726th Regiment, 716th Division, held the Pointe.

The battle plan was this: At the precise moment that the two combat teams were landing at Omaha Beach, three companies of the 2nd Rangers would attack Pointe du Hoc from the sea. They would come in under an umbrella of bombardment by the battleship *Texas* and two destroyers, the *Satterlee* and the British destroyer, *Talybont*.

The main Ranger force, comprising two more companies from the 2nd Battalion and the entire 5th Battalion, would wait offshore for a signal of success, then land at the Pointe to reinforce the assault team. The Ranger group would then move inland, cut the coastal highway connecting the towns of Vierville and Grandcamp, and await the arrival of the 116th Infantry before pushing onward.

The assault team, led by Lt. Col. James E. Rudder, had only half an hour to take the Pointe. If, by 7:00 A.M., he had not sent his signal to the Rangers waiting offshore, that group would proceed to land at "Beach Dog Green" behind the 116th Infantry, advance through them overland, and attack the Pointe from the landward side.

Company C, 2nd Rangers, had a separate mission of its own at Omaha Beach. It was ordered to land with the first assault wave of the 116th and knock out German strong points near Pointe de la Percée, on the immediate right flank of Omaha Beach.

On June 6th, at 4:45 A.M., as the main body of the invasion force headed for the beaches, a small flotilla of Rangers set off on its own dangerous mission. Ten landing crafts held Ranger Companies D, E, and F and Col. Rudder's headquarters group—about twenty-one men in each boat. The other craft held equipment and supplies.

Each landing craft was fitted with three pairs of rocket mounts, carrying rope ladders. The rockets were headed by grapnels. When fired from a control point at the stern, the rockets would reach the top of the cliff. The grapnels would catch, and the men would go up the ladders. Each craft also carried an extension ladder consisting of 112 feet of tubular steel, in 16-foot sections. To mount it, a man would climb 16 feet, haul up and attach the grapnels to the next section, then repeat the process until he reached the top.

As a final aid, four amphibious trucks, called "ducks," would come in close behind the first wave, each carrying a 100-foot extension ladder borrowed from the London Fire Brigade.

Shortly after leaving their transports, the landing craft began to suffer from the rough seas. Eight miles from shore, one boat was swamped by a large wave, spilling Capt. Harold K. Slater and twenty men from Company D into the water. They were eventually rescued, but were in no condition to fight. Ten minutes later, one of the supply boats sank, with only one survivor. The other supply craft was soon in trouble and had to jettison all the packs of Companies D and E in order to remain afloat. The other boats were taking in so much water that the men were forced to bail out with their helmets in order to help the pumps.

Still, the nine remaining assault craft kept good formation as they neared the shore. Then the lead boat lost its bearings and headed straight for Pointe de la Percée, three miles east of its target. When Col. Rudder realized the error, he shouted to the coxswain to change course. The damage had been done, however. The mistake cost more than thirty minutes in reaching Pointe du Hoc; instead of attacking at 6:30 A.M., the Rangers touched down at 7:08. By then, Lt. Col. Max Schneider, in command of the 500 Rangers waiting offshore, should have had his success signal. Rudder was supposed to fire flares as soon as his men had scaled the cliffs. Hearing nothing from Rudder, Schneider ordered his men to go in at Beach Dog Green. Rudder's three companies would have to fight alone on the Pointe.

The delay and misdirection had further results. Swinging back toward Pointe du Hoc, the Ranger flotilla passed parallel to the shore. Therefore, they ran the gauntlet of fire from German guns along the three-mile coast. Luckily, most of the fire was haphazard. But one "duck" was destroyed by shellfire, killing five of the men on board.

Finally, the delay cost the Rangers their covering naval gunfire. The ships stopped bombarding the Pointe just before 6:30. That gave the Germans on the cliff forty minutes to recover and reorganize. When the nine landing craft scraped to a halt at the edge of the beach, the Germans were ready for them. A shower of grenades and the clatter of machine guns greeted the Rangers.

Rudder's boat was the first to hit the beach. Here, unlike the beaches at Omaha, naval gunfire and aerial bombardment had created deep craters in the sand. The men found themselves neck-deep in water, trying to dodge bullets and grenades. Rudder found a shallow cave at the base of the cliff, where he set up a command post.

The rockets were fired from Rudder's boat. Some of the waterlogged ropes reached the top. The men dragged out an extension ladder and placed it against the cliff. Then they began to clamber up, firing at the Germans on the top. Sgt. Dominick Boggetto sprayed the cliff face with his BAR. Two Germans toppled off the edge and fell to the rocks below. The rest scattered.

Now the other assault boats scraped in. A wild, confused battle began. The Rangers fired their rockets. Some grapnels caught, and some of the ropes were long enough, but the Germans popped out of their clifftop

A German soldier stands guard duty beside a huge German gun commanding the sea at Omaha Beach.

trenches, cut the ropes, threw grenades, fired their *Schmeisser* submachine guns at the climbing Rangers, and took shelter again.

The Rangers scrambled from their boats, thrashed about in the water-filled shell holes, started up the rope ladders, and fired as they climbed. Some men, impatient with ropes and ladders, cut hand and foot holds in the face of the cliff and began scrambling toward the top. Snipers picked off many of them, their bodies tumbling down into the sea.

Offshore, the skippers of the *Satterlee* and the *Talybont* saw the meleé and realized the plight of the Rangers. "They're pinned under the cliff! They're being cut to pieces!" exclaimed Commander Marshall on board the *Satterlee*. The destroyer immediately opened up on the German positions with its 5-inch guns and 40mm machine guns. The skipper of the *Talybont* moved in closer to shore and raked the top of the cliff with the ship's 2-inch and 4-inch guns.

The naval gunfire sent the Germans scurrying to the protection of their trenches and bunkers. But the men on the destroyers also noticed that huge chunks of earth and rock were being blasted out of the cliff face and were falling on the climbing Rangers. The destroyers backed off.

The brief respite was enough. All over the face of the cliff men were slithering up ropes and ladders, boosting themselves over the cratered edge, taking on the German defenders. Cpl. Ed Smith slung his carbine over his shoulder, grabbed a hanging rope and "walked it up" the side of the cliff. Flinging himself over the top, he saw a group of Germans throwing grenades over the cliff. He shot one of them. The rest turned and fired back at him. He ducked into a shell hole.

Sgt. Hayward Robey jumped in beside him with a BAR. Fast firing, the two men sprayed the group of

German grenadiers with forty or fifty rounds. Three of the grenadiers were killed. The rest disappeared into shelters. Pfc. Frank Petersen, wounded by a grenade, joined the two Rangers, and the three men advanced on the German positions without waiting for the other climbers.

Now Rangers were everywhere, climbing over the edges of the cliff. At the very tip of the Pointe, S. Sgt. Charles H. Denbo and Pvt. Harry Roberts found themselves about twenty feet from a massive and undamaged concrete observation post. Roberts crawled toward a trench. At once, rifle and machine gun fire started up from slits in the OP. The Rangers threw four grenades at the slits. Three went in. The guns stopped firing, but not before Denbo was wounded by a bullet. Four more Rangers joined Denbo and Roberts, including Sgt. Andrew J. Yardley, toting a bazooka. Yardley slammed two shells through the firing slit, killing any Germans still alive.

At 7:45, Col. Rudder moved his command post to a shell crater near the top of the cliff. Capt. Walter E. Block, the battalion surgeon, remained below with the wounded. Thus far, the two Ranger companies had about fifty casualties. Before the day was out, Rudder's 225-man force would be cut to 90. And, ironically, it was a futile battle.

The sight greeting the Rangers on top of Pointe du Hoc reminded some of them of scenes from World War I films, depicting "No-Man's Land." The ground was a shattered wasteland, torn to pieces by bombs and heavy naval shells. Craters and mounds of wreckage scarred the landscape. Not a landmark was recognizable. For months, the Rangers had studied maps and aerial photographs of the Pointe du Hoc fortifications. Now, holes and piles of debris obscured everything.

One thing, however, was quite clear. There were no

This was a German Observation Post, set on a hill overlooking Omaha Beach.

Men of the 2nd Ranger Battalion plant the U.S. flag for recognition and lead German prisoners off Pointe du Hoc.

big guns on Pointe du Hoc. The positions were pulverized, the concrete casements badly damaged. But there was no sign of the guns themselves. Evidently, the 155's had been removed from the Pointe long before the invasion bombardment had begun. All had been in vain.

At Beach Dog Green, Company C of the 2nd Battalion went in with the first wave of troops from the 116th Regimental Combat Team. Commanded by Capt. Ralph E. Goranson, they were in two assault boats, thirty-four men to a boat. Most of the men became seasick in the choppy waters. Then, nearing shore, one of the two boats was hit twice by artillery shells. Ten men were killed, several more seriously wounded. When the boats ground to a halt and the ramps came down, the emerging men were cut down by machine gun fire.

Capt. Goranson led his surviving band across 300 yards of open beach to the shelter at the base of the cliff. He had thirty men left, five of whom were wounded.

The Fifth Battalion and the rest of the 2nd Battalion, under Col. Schneider, were more fortunate. When Schneider failed to get the required success signal from Col. Rudder at the Pointe by 7:10 A.M. he sent his force of Rangers toward Beach Dog Green, according to plan. But when he saw that the Germans were turning Dog Green into a slaughterhouse, he took his force half a mile down the assault area to Beach Dog White. Here, they got off their boats and onto the beach area with relatively few casualties.

One of the first men on shore was Capt. Joe Rafferty, commanding Company A, 2nd Rangers. Just a few days before, he had been promoted from lieutenant. Wading ashore, he was hit in the legs by a spray of machine gun bullets. Behind him, his men hesitated. Staggering to his feet, he waved his men forward, aware that staying on the

33

A mortar crew in action on "Beach Dog Green."

beach was suicide. Shouting and waving his arms, he got all his men off the boat and running for the protection of the seawall. As the last man passed him, Rafferty turned to follow. But it was too late. A shell from a German 88 exploded near him, killing him instantly.

As the morning wore on, the American situation at Omaha Beach did not look encouraging. On Pointe du Hoc, Rudder and his Rangers were being harassed by snipers and artillery fire. They were gaining ground, but the little force was being chipped away, bit by bit.

Capt. Goranson and his band were pinned down by intensive enemy machine gun fire. They couldn't move.

Omaha Beach presented a dismaying picture of death and destruction. A pall of black smoke hung over the area. Burning, smoldering vehicles and boats lay at the water's edge. Wreckage was piled upon wreckage. Bodies floated gently on the rising tide. Along the shoreline, medics performed heroic miracles among the wounded, but their Red Cross armbands and helmet insignia were no protection against bullets and shells.

Aboard the command ship *Augusta*, Gen. Omar Bradley gravely studied the reports coming in from Omaha Beach. He began to wonder about the attack. He thought perhaps it would be best to get the survivors off, abandon the beachhead, and push the assault on Utah Beach—a more successful endeavor. In the end, he decided to wait a bit longer. He had confidence in his subordinate commanders, and in the men of his divisions.

Now, on those bloody beaches, Bradley's confidence was beginning to pay off. Ignoring the bullets kicking up sand all around them, senior officers, such as Col. Taylor and Col. Canham, coolly urged their men forward, off the death trap beaches.

Along Dog Green and Dog White, Gen. Cota walked up and down calmly, waving his .45 pistol about, urging his men to get up off their bellies and follow him into the fight. Spying a group of Rangers crouching behind a seawall, he waved to them and called out, "Lead the way, Rangers!"

It was like a spark that set the men on fire.

4
The Tide Turns

A platoon of Col. Schneider's Rangers scrambled over the seawall, blew gaps in the barbed wire, and charged up the hill. An enemy machine gun swept across the line of men. The line hesitated, took the shock, then pressed on. Lt. Francis Dawson, the platoon leader, led a squad of men in a flanking movement. With grenades and bayonets they wiped out the machine gun nest. Dawson waved his men forward. Soon, the rest of the company followed. Then the battalion advanced through a honeycomb of mines toward their destination: the road to Vierville.

All along Omaha Beach, soldiers rose from the sand and began to move forward, firing their weapons as they advanced. Machine gunners set up their weapons and returned the fire of the German machine gunners on the bluffs. Bazooka teams blasted away at pillboxes and bunkers. Small groups of men, without officers or squad leaders, formed combat teams of their own. A few tanks rumbled down the ramps of newly arrived landing craft and added their cannons to the growing gunfire.

Slowly, yard by yard, the men fought their way off Bloody Omaha.

Sgt. Phil Streczyk, of E Company, 16th Regimental Combat Team, found himself on the beach with thirty-two men from his section. This was the company that had lost most of its officers and 105 men in the water. Ahead of Streczyk were 300 yards of sand and a steep hill. On the right side of the hill, Streczyk could see fire coming from a German bunker. Around the bunker were riflemen firing down at the beach.

Streczyk knew he had to get his men off the beach or they would all be picked off, one by one. "Get going!" he yelled. "A couple of guys at a time! We'll cover you!"

Setting up a line of rifle fire, Streczyk sent his men forward. At the base of the hill was a small ravine, and it was toward this defense that he directed the men. The first two made it safely and took cover. When the next pair went, one was shot down, the other got across safely. The next two ran across the beach, zigzagging to avoid the enemy fire. Halfway across, both men stepped on mines. Their bodies flew into the air. Both were killed instantly.

It took an hour for Streczyk and his section to get across to the ravine. Counting heads, the sergeant saw he had twenty men left of the thirty-two he'd started with. Leading them up the ravine, Streczyk got to the crest of the hill and found that he had outflanked the German bunker and connecting trenches. Fourteen Germans in the trenches were caught flat-footed. Streczyk and his men blazed away with rifles and submachine guns. Twelve of the Germans were killed. Two surrendered.

The men then attacked the concrete bunker. Throwing grenades and firing their one bazooka, the men moved in to encircle the strong point. The Germans fired back with machine guns. More Germans ran up to counterattack. Streczyk and his men took over the German trenches

Assault troops of the 16th Infantry take cover as a German 88 hits the beach near them.

and set up a withering cross fire. Ten more Germans fell. A few more shouted "Kamerad!" and surrendered. But the bunker continued its rapid machine gun fire.

Analyzing the predicament, Streczyk realized he hadn't enough men or fire power to knock out the German strong point. But he could "put it on ice," or neutralize it. So he deployed his men on the hill in positions from where they could keep the bunker under fire while being well protected themselves. He sent a few men back to the beach with the prisoners, blew gaps in the barbed wire leading up the hill, and strung tape along the beach where his men had been killed by the mines, as a warning to others.

Streczyk's bold action did much to clear the way for the following waves of 1st Division men landing on the beach. He was later awarded the Silver Star for bravery.

When Capt. Ettore Zappacosta of Company B, 116th RCT, was killed while wading toward the beach, command of the company went to Lt. William B. Williams. A mortar shell hit his boat dead center just as the men were leaving it. Williams led his surviving group in a dash, to the protection of a seawall. More men fell while crossing the beach. At the wall, Williams had only ten men left.

Pinned down for about half an hour by machine gun and mortar fire, Williams, too, realized that the men must advance and attack or be wiped out on the beach. Ordering his men to give him covering fire, Williams charged the machine gun nest by himself, a live grenade in each hand. He hadn't gone three yards before he was hit. As he fell, he threw the grenades. They exploded too far away from the gun nest to do any damage. Undaunted, he crawled forward, pulling the pin from another grenade. Two more bullets hit him. He threw the grenade. This time it fell into the machine gun pit, killing the crew and silencing the gun.

Staggering to his feet, Williams waved his men forward. Mortar fire fell among them. Spotting the enemy gun, Williams crawled to a flanking position so he could throw his grenade. The enemy saw him. Their grenades exploded all around him. Shrapnel hit him, wounding him for the third time. Bleeding badly, he inched forward. When close enough, he threw two grenades at the mortar and killed the crew.

Then, calling to his men, Williams turned over his map and compass to S. Sgt. Frank Price. "You men keep going toward Vierville," he said. "I can't move. I'll hang on here."

The medics didn't find Williams until nightfall. Miraculously, he was still alive. For his extraordinary heroism, Williams was awarded the Distinguished Service Cross.

Over on Dog Red Beach, the Germans were still creating hell. The headquarters' boats of the 2nd Battalion, the 116th RCT, had taken a terrific beating. The battalion supply officer, Capt. Sherman Burroughs, was killed as he left his boat. Capt. Robert DeWitt, the battalion surgeon, fell with shrapnel wounds in the face and leg. Five medics were killed, and the chaplain, Capt. Charles Reed, was wounded. As Maj. Sydney Bingham, the battalion commander, led his men toward the shelter of the seawall, an artillery shell landed. One large shard from it cut half of S. Sgt. Arthur Woods' neck away and killed him instantly. Another piece of shrapnel cut through both cheeks of Capt. Charles Cawthon. Because he was talking, the piece of steel missed his jaw. The blood dribbled down his face and over his shirt, but Capt. Cawthon finished giving his orders before seeking a medic.

Company E had also taken a beating. Casualties in the water and on the beach were heavy. The Company Commander, Capt. Lawrence A. Madill, was wounded.

Around him, the grim survivors of his company awaited his orders. He found that his entire mortar section had been killed except for one man, Pfc. Walter Masterly. And although he had his mortar, he had no ammunition for it. Masterly volunteered to go back to the beach and salvage some ammunition, but the captain said, "No, I'll go. You set up your gun."

Dodging machine gun and sniper fire, the captain went back to his assault boat. Finding the ammunition, he picked some up and headed back for Masterly's position. This time the German machine guns didn't miss. Already wounded, he went down, got up, was hit again, and fell to the sand. His last words were, "Senior noncom, take the men off the beach!"

Sgt. Maurice Hatchett and Sgt. Lionel Patterson assumed command and began moving the men forward. As they did so, an enemy pillbox, about 300 yards to the left, sprayed the men with machine gun fire. Two men dropped, mortally wounded. Grabbing a bazooka, Sgt. Hatchett fired two rounds at the pillbox. Despite the long range, both shells struck home. The machine gun stopped firing.

Ahead of the men now was a row of barbed wire. Pfc. Porter Boggis stepped forward and cut open a path. The two sergeants rushed through, followed by about fifty men. More machine guns fired at them, and the men took cover in a ditch. Bullets kicked up little puffs of dust all around them. For the moment, the men were stuck. Directly in front of them was a clearly marked mine field. They couldn't advance; on the other hand, the German machine gunners, firing down from a vantage point on a hill above the ditch, were getting the range. One man was hit, then another. Finally, Pvt. Jack Kerber got up and ran forward with a bangalore torpedo, hoping to blow a path through the mine field. But he stepped on a mine and was blown to bits.

Reinforcements pour ashore on Omaha Beach. This photo was taken from a hill only moments before it was taken from the Germans.

Suddenly, Sgt. Patterson noticed a thin strand of wire along the edge of the ditch where he'd taken cover. From his training, he realized that this was how the Germans marked the boundary of a mine field for their own men. Setting up a BAR to give covering fire, Sgt. Patterson got his men out of the ditch and through the mine field. Near the crest of the hill, his group ran into cross fire from two machine guns.

Telling his men to take cover, Sgt. Patterson went after the guns himself. Skirting the brow of the hill, he came across the first gun. Boldly stepping forward in full view, he wiped out the machine gun nest with his submachine gun. Then, retracing his steps, he crept around to the other side of the hill. There, he found the other machine gun. The Germans were busy moving it to fire at Patterson's men below. Sgt. Patterson quickly threw two grenades at the position. As they exploded, he charged the gun and, with a burst from his Thompson, he made sure no Germans survived.

Patterson then stood on the brow of the hill and waved to his men to come forward. For his heroism, Sgt. Patterson was given the Distinguished Service Cross.

Company F of the 16th RCT, 1st Division, had only two officers who were able to fight, it should be remembered. One of these was the company commander, Capt. John Finke. But leading an attack on a mortar position, Finke was wounded. Under the circumstances, that left the fate of the company up to the sergeants. One of these was S. Sgt. Raymond F. Strojny. His platoon leader, Lt. Otto Clemens, had been killed while leading his men off the landing boat. Most of the other men in the section had been either killed or wounded when they crossed the beach to the seawall. The medic, Pvt. Morris T. Levine, although seriously wounded himself, helped many of the wounded to safety before he collapsed. He was awarded the Silver Star.

Sgt. Strojny found himself with only seven unwounded men. Machine gun bullets were flying everywhere. For about twenty minutes, the men remained behind the seawall, their heads tucked into their helmets, frozen to the spot. Finally, Sgt. Strojny had had enough. Leaping over the seawall, he found a trench from which he could fire his M1. He called to the men to join him. They scrambled over the wall and fell in beside him. He pointed out two enemy machine gun positions. Setting up a firing line, Sgt. Strojny and the men poured in a steady stream of fire, silencing the machine guns. A few moments later, the little group was joined by a sergeant and a few men from the 116th RCT who had landed on the wrong beach. The sergeant was carrying a bazooka.

"Just what we need," said Sgt. Strojny. He pointed to a concrete gun emplacement, 100 yards away, that was firing a 75mm gun at the landing beaches.

"I need somebody to load for me," said the sergeant.

"I'll do it," said Sgt. Strojny.

The sergeant fired two rounds at the gun. Both missed. Just then, a mortar round exploded near the two men. Sgt. Strojny was unhurt, but the other sergeant was severely wounded. The bazooka was holed by shell fragments. Nevertheless, Sgt. Strojny picked it up and fired it. His first two rounds missed. The next two hit the concrete emplacement. But the gun kept firing. Thoroughly angry, Sgt. Strojny yelled for more ammunition. But there was none.

Strojny ran back to the beach, rummaged around the wreckage, and found six bazooka shells. Dodging enemy bullets, he brought the shells back to his position, grabbed the bazooka, and fired all six rounds. The first five had no effect, but the sixth apparently went right through the

Troops of the 29th swing an anti-tank gun into action behind Omaha Beach, as German Tigers move in to counter-attack.

firing slit and hit the ammunition inside. The pillbox went up in flames.

Seeing the fire, Sgt. Strojny urged his men forward. He got up and ran toward the position, but nobody followed him. When Strojny saw a German soldier running from the pillbox, he took aim with his M1 and shot him down. As he did so, a sniper shot at Strojny. The bullet entered his helmet over his left eye, dug a furrow through the skin along his scalp, and punctured a large hole in the rear of the helmet. With blood dripping down the side of his face, Sgt. Strojny stood his gound and called to his men once again. They came forward this time, and Sgt. Strojny led them up a hill toward a wooded area. When barbed wire fence stopped them, a man from the 116th stepped forward with a bangalore torpedo and blew a hole in the wire.

Ordering his men to hold back, Sgt. Strojny carefully went ahead and found a path through the mine field. On the other side, he waved the men forward. Five men from his own section, as well as a lieutenant and a squad from the 116th, ran through the wire and across the mine field to join him. The group immediately came under machine gun fire from their right flank. Deploying themselves in a skirmish line, the men ran toward the machine gun, firing their rifles and submachine guns. They wiped out the machine gun nest and killed seven Germans.

Sgt. Strojny then wanted to keep on going, right into the wooded area that lay before them. But the lieutenant cautioned that it would be better to wait until artillery could be brought up to shell the woods. Strojny gathered the few men that remained about him, and took off to find any other survivors from his company. For his outstanding action, he was awarded the Distinguished Service Cross.

This was the pattern set along Omaha Beach as the

German anti-tank gunners in action behind Omaha Beach on D-Day.

afternoon wore on. Amid the havoc and confusion, brave men—officers, sergeants, privates—broke the German grip on the beach area. Now the Germans were taking it on the chin. The grenadiers of the 716th and 352nd Divisions were being pushed back, back across the bluffs, back toward the key towns of Colleville and Vierville. Keyed-up GI's, thirsting for revenge for their buddies slaughtered on the beaches, advanced across the fields, gunning down everything in their path. Behind them they left burning pillboxes, shattered bunkers, and entrenchments filled with dead Germans. Columns of prisoners began to file down the bluffs to the beaches.

At 1:30 P.M., Gen. Bradley got an all clear message from Omaha Beach: "Units formerly pinned down are now advancing on all fronts toward their objectives."

Company C of the 116th, more fortunate than most, was one of the units well prepared for the afternoon's advance. Their boats had landed at a section of the beach where a grass fire on the bluffs above had been started by naval gunfire. The thick smoke gave the boats some protection from the German guns, but a few men were killed, and a few were wounded, including the Company Commander, Capt. Bertier Hawks.

Lt. Stanley Schwartz took over and led the men to the seawall. With heavy 88 fire coming down around them, the lieutenant decided to take a chance and fight his way up the bluffs. He found a hole in the seawall and led his men through. They were stopped short by a double apron of barbed wire. Pvt. Engram E. Lambert crawled forward with a bangalore torpedo, but machine gun fire killed him before he could light the fuse. Then Lt. Schwartz set off the torpedo and blew a gap in the wire.

The lieutenant barely waited for the smoke to settle before he was off and running through the gap. The rest of the men followed him through a hail of artillery and

With the beach secured, men of a heavy weapons unit begin to move inland.

machine gun fire. Two men were killed and six were wounded before the men found some abandoned trenches and jumped in them.

After resting until the enemy fire abated, Lt. Schwartz got his men up and out of the trenches. Shaping them into proper platoons, he deployed them across the fields and advanced along a road leading to Vierville. This group may have fought the most organized company actions of the day.

Half a mile from Vierville, the company came under fire from two machine guns. Lt. Schwartz took a platoon and a mortar section and deployed to the left to outflank the guns, while the rest of the company gave covering fire. The guns appeared to be positioned behind a hedge. The lieutenant's platoon reached within thirty yards of the first gun without seeing it. Then the machine gun began firing. Lt. Schwartz, S. Sgt. Ted Mouray, and Pfc. Leo King were killed by the first burst. The rest of the platoon fired at the hedge. When the German gun ceased firing, the platoon edged forward and found that the gunner was dead.

Then the second machine gun opened up. Quickly, the rest of the company closed in on it and, with a shower of grenades, eliminated the second gun. Then, with 1st Sgt. Alfred B. McClure in the lead, the men continued their advance to Vierville.

Cautiously, they entered the town, searching for snipers, wary of hidden machine gun emplacements. All was quiet. As they reached the main square, the men were astonished to find Gen. Cota standing there, calmly twirling his pistol on his finger.

He grinned at them. "Where the hell have you been, boys?" he said.

5
The End of the Beginning

In the little French village of La Roche-Guyon, many miles behind the invasion beaches, Maj. Gen. Hans Speidel pounded his fist on the desk in front of him and swore softly. Speidel was Rommel's Chief of Staff, and the news he was getting on the telephone was not good. Furthermore, he fretted about the responsibility he had not asked for, just because Rommel had picked these few days to go home to Ulm for a brief rest. The Field Marshal had been so sure there would be no invasion this week because of the weather, that he had left Speidel in charge of the headquarters of Army Group B, the most powerful German force in France.

Now, alerted by Speidel, Rommel was on the way back by car. But it would be many hours before his return; the roads were hazardous, and American and British fighter planes strafed every moving vehicle. Meanwhile, there were decisions to be made. Speidel was in constant touch with the generals at the front: Richter of the 716th, Kraiss of the 352nd in the American zone, Reichert of the 711th, and Feuchtinger of the 21st Panzers in the British sector.

In the beginning, during the first hour or two of the invasion, it had looked as though the Allies would be driven back into the sea. This was particularly true at Omaha Beach. Reports from Richter and Kraiss had spoken of burning ships, smashed tanks, and thousands of American casualties. They had sounded so confident of victory. But now, in the waning hours of the afternoon, Richter reported that his division was almost wiped out, reduced to a few ragged companies. The Americans were sweeping forward all along the front. He had nothing left. Kraiss's division, the 352nd, was also smashed.

Speidel had pleaded for reinforcements immediately. But, back at *Oberkommando West*, the German Army's supreme headquarters, Col. Gen. Alfred Jodl and his deputy, Gen. Walter Warlimont, hesitated for a few hours. Then they sent forward two of the Wermacht's veteran divisions, the *S.S. Panzer Lehr* and the *12th S.S.* But it was too late—far too late.

Speidel, at his desk in the castle of La Roche-Guyon, knew this. He realized that by the time those two crack S.S. divisions arrived at the front, the Americans would have a secure toehold. But it was too late to stop the invasion.

When Rommel arrived that evening, both generals calmly surveyed the situation and understood that all was lost.

Colored pins on the map told the story. The key coastal towns of Coleville and Vierville were securely in the hands of the 1st and 29th Divisions. The Rangers of Col. Max Schneider and Capt. Ralph Goranson had outflanked the Germans holding the Vierville-St. Laurent road. They had killed or captured scores of Germans and linked up with Col. Rudder's men on Pointe du Hoc. The

American wounded, lined up on the deck of a landing craft that will transport them to a hospital in England.

German soldiers examine the wreckage of an American glider, shot down during the pre-dawn Airborne Division attacks on D-Day.

dreaded 155mm howitzers had been found hidden in a wood and destroyed.

Except for a few German snipers remaining stubbornly in the area, Omaha Beach was clear. Landing crafts bulled their way right up onto the sands through huge gaps blown through the obstacles by the engineers. Tons of equipment piled up on the beach—much-needed rations and ammunition. Artillery rolled off other landing crafts—75's and 105's, 37mm anti-tank guns, and Sherman tanks of the 743rd Tank Battalion. More boats were bringing in troops by the thousands—the 18th and 26th Regiments of the 1st Division, and the 115th and 175th Regiments of the 29th Division.

As the sun began to settle slowly beneath the sea on the night of June 6th, weary GI's dug foxholes and settled in for a few moments of precious sleep. Tomorrow and for eleven months of tomorrows, there would be bitter fighting and tens of thousands more casualties before Hitler was dead and Germany defeated.

But for now, at least, the mission had been accomplished and the GI's could rest. The beachhead was safe. Not without cost, however. Each of the two assaulting regimental combat teams (the 16th and the 116th) lost about 1,000 men on D-Day.

They are not forgotten. To this very day, a memorial stands on that beach. In the cemetery nearby, on each anniversary of D-Day, French people from the villages of Normandy put flowers on the graves of those gallant GI's who fell so that they might be free of the Nazi yoke.

And from America, many of those veterans of the 16th and 116th, who lived through the holocaust of World War II, also come on the 6th of June, to pay their respects to buddies who died that day on Bloody Omaha.

Index

Bert, Pfc. George, 19
Bingham, Maj. Sydney, 41
Block, Capt. Walter E., 30
Boggetto, Sgt. Dominick, 27
Boggis, Pfc. Porter, 42
Bradley, Gen. Omar, 35, 49
Burroughs, Capt. Sherman, 41

Canham, Col. Charles, 19, 35
Cathon, Capt. Charles, 41
Chase, Sgt. Rodney, 17
Clemens, Lt. Otto, 44
Colleville, 49, 53
Cota, Brig. Gen. Norman D., 21, 35, 51

Dallas, Lt. Tom, 15
Dawson, Lt. Francis, 37
DeBellis, Pfc. Frank, 19
Denbo, S. Sgt. Charles H., 30
Dennstedt, Lt. Aaron, 17
DeWitt, Capt. Robert, 41

Eisenhower, Gen. Dwight D., 3

Finke, Capt. John, 44

Goranson, Capt. Ralph E., 33, 53
Grandcamp, 25

Hatchett, Sgt. Maurice, 42
Hawks, Capt. Bertier, 49

Hitler, Adolph, 2, 3, 9

Jodl, Col. Gen. Alfred, 53

Kerber, Pvt. Jack, 42
King, Pfc. Leo, 31

Lambert, Pvt. Engram E., 49
Levine, Pvt. Morris T., 44-5

Madill, Capt. Laurence A., 41-2
Masterly, Pfc. Walter, 52
McClure, 1st Sgt. Alfred B., 51
Miller, S. Sgt. William A., 17
Mouray, S. Sgt. Ted, 51

Nance, Lt. Elijah, 15
Nash, Pvt. Leo J., 14

Patterson, Sgt. Lionel, 42, 44
Pearre, Lt. Howard, 17
Petersen, Pfc. Frank, 30
Pointe de la Percée, 25-6
Pointe du Hoc, 23, 25-7, 30, 33, 35, 53
Price, S. Sgt. Frank, 41
Price, Sgt. Robert, 17

Rafferty, Capt. Joe, 33, 35
Reed, Capt. Charles, 41
Roberts, Pvt. Harry, 30
Robey, Sgt. Hayward, 29

Roche-Guyon, La, 52-3
Rommel, Field Marshal Erwin, 5, 9, 52-3
Rudder, Lt. Col. James E., 25-7, 30, 33, 53
Rush, Lt. Bernard J., 19

Sales, Pfc. Robert L., 15
Schneider, Col. Max, 26-7, 33, 37, 53
Schwartz, Lt. Stanley, 49, 51
Slater, Capt. Harold K., 26
Smith, Cpl. Ed., 29
Speidel, Maj. Gen. Hans, 52-3
Streczyk, Sgt. Phil, 38, 40
Strojny, S. Sgt. Raymond, 44-5, 47

Taylor, Col. George A., 21, 35
Tellers, Capt. Taylor N., 14
Tidrick, Lt. Edward, 14

Vierville, 25, 49, 51, 53

Warlimont, Gen. Walter, 53
Williams, Lt. William B., 40-1
Woods, S. Sgt. Arthur, 41

Yardley, Sgt. Andrew J., 30

Zappacosta, Capt. Ettore V., 15, 40